A CASE AGAINST WAR
The Imperative of Love and the
Unsustainability of Peace

CHARLES MWEWA

Copyright © 2024 Charles Mwewa

www.charlesmwewa.com

Published by:

ACP

Ottawa, ON Canada

www.acpress.ca

www.springopus.com

info@acpress.ca

All rights reserved.

ISBN: 978-1-998788-64-4

DEDICATION

For the victims of war, everywhere!

CONTENTS

DEDICATION iii
CONTENTS v
AUTHOR'S WORDS vii
1 | IRRATIONALITY OF WAR 1
2 | IRRELEVANCE OF WAR 5
    Assumption 1: 9
    Assumption 2: 9
    Assumption 3: 10
    Assumption 4: 11
    Assumption 5: 12
    Assumption 6: 12
    Assumption 7: 13
    Assumption 8: 14
3 | IRRESPONSIBILITY OF WAR 15
7 | IRRESPOSABILITY OF WAR 23
    ABOUT THE AUTHOR 31
    SELECTED BOOKS BY THIS AUTHOR 33
    INDEX 39

AUTHOR'S WORDS

War. The dictionary defines it as a state of armed conflict between different nations or states or different groups within a nation or state. A conflict is defined as a serious and protracted disagreement or argument. Armed is defined as equipped with or carrying a weapon or weapons.

So, war may candidly be defined as being engaged in a serious and protracted disagreement or argument with weapons, between different nations or states or different groups within a nation or state.

There is no good war or wars. All wars involve the use of aggression and weapons. Aggression is hostility, anger, violence, or assault. Weapons may include other weapons other than guns, firearms, munitions, ammunition, etc.

No-one wins in a war. The benefits of war are hugely outweighed by the detriments of love. Nations and peoples and groups should not make war, but love, for then *this* world, will be a better place.

c.m.

1 | IRRATIONALITY OF WAR

Elements of War

Nations go to war, mostly, for three reasons: Patriotism; love/hate; or revenge. These three reasons are what we may called the Elements of War. When a nation has been provoked, through aggression or threats, it may resort to war. In doing so, it may be attempting to satisfy all the three elements in one action. To make it easier for nations, inaction by the authorities may be construed by the general public as betrayal. So, some governments may be under pressure to declare war.

Irrationality of Sentimental Conveyance

No matter the justification or reason for war, the declaration of war is an irrational conveyance of national sentiments. Motives may be personal or sectarian, but those empowered to make decisions on war may be imprisoned by the reasonableness of not declaring war, usually, owing to political or social pressure. The three elements of war may be used as basis for the declaration of war, and, indirectly, labeling those who opposite such sentiments as unpatriotic, or non-lovers of the state.

The sentimentality of war is overtly overrated due to overriding emotional presuppositions. Thus, the governors and the governed may demand war and then evaluate its consequences later. History and commonsense have provided ample examples of the irrationality of war. When wars are fought, they begin as a justification for one of the three elements. But when wars end, temporally or permanently, the consequences almost always outweigh the motives or elemental factors.

Far-Reaching Consequences

War is a boomerang; it first devastates the opposition before it turns on the declarant. The direct impact of war may be death of people from both sides. However, the permanent impact of war is far-reaching. Only war itself wins; humans lose. Because war does not end *per se*, it can only be silenced for few years. Once those whose ancestors died in war begin to review history, they may be left with only one response, to view revenge as panacea for historical injustices or pain or embarrassment, or all of the three.

Provocation & Declaration of War

The best way to deal with war, is not to provoke or declare it. Both provocation and declaration of war trigger indefensible emotions. These emotions may be temporary, but they might have ushered in permanent aggression and the resolution to battles to settle disputes. The one who provokes war and the one who declares it may both be irrational – they may be blinded by hate, so-called patriotic feelings or a quest for vengeance – but in the end, they might have simply been overwhelmed by pressure or emotions.

Decisions to declare war or to go to war must not be made, and if made, they must not be made lightly. Because when they are made, the present and the future suffer, no matter the justification.

War is irrational.

2 | IRRELEVANCE OF WAR

No Intrinsic Value

War has no intrinsic or lasting value. Its purpose is often revenge. Revenge is not justice. Revenge is reprisal or payback. Revenge is a volatile reaction, and it is irrational at best. No-one wins by getting revenge against another. When one or a nation carries out revenge, it becomes the aggressor instead of being a victim.

Survivors will usually demand revenge. It is expected, and it sounds reasonable. But in the end, survivors are not honored because their government took revenge. The dead may even be offended. If the dead are to be considered, they may have a say, a voice of reason, that of not resorting to vengeance. Once they die, they may be in a better position to view things holistically and choose non-vengeful reactions.

However, the problem is that the dead do not have a say in the matters of the living. Rational people must speak for the dead. They must insist on keeping bargain by not carrying out revenge. Revenge preempts eternal blessings.

Lives lost may not be capable of retribution. But true retribution is in keeping the good memory of the dead rather than in carrying out vengeful missions supposedly on behalf of the dead.

Historically Unjustified

War is historically unjustified. Past wars have never solved what was supposedly the reasons for war in the first place. Consider the First World War and the Second World War. What benefits came from these wars? Consider ancient wars, what did they accomplish. All those who declared or participated in them are both long dead. And then who won, they both died, eventually?

War is insanity.

Patriotism is not usually compensable for lost opportunities. Some people think that they are very patriotic if they carry out vengeful missions on behalf of their nations. War has no value; it makes people forget what is true and noble.

Those who remain (survivors) suffer more pain, loss, regret, trauma and are inconvenienced more than those who perish, on both sides. No side truly wins, even if they may raise the victory flag.

No Moral Justification

War has never been right because there are no right outcomes. Take the war between Russia and Ukraine, while Russia might have an upper hand, it lost favor with the rest of the international community. Ukraine, on the other hand, suffered irreparable damage to infrastructure and lost and displaced lives.

Consider Hamas war against Israel, while Hamas might have thought that it was meting out historical vengeance, in the end, it suffered massive destruction to its city and human life. Israel, on the other hand, may never recuperate from regional targeting and insecurity. What caused all this, war.

War is immoral.

Innocent people suffer during and after the war has ended, even more than the combatants and generals and those who authorized the war. When it is announced that one side has won the war, it should also be announced that the other side has not lost the war. Or when it is announced that one side has lost the war, it should also be announced that the other side has not won the war.

War has no winners.

Hate has never conquered hate, only love conquers hate. War cannot be fought without the backing of hatred. Combatants must hate one another to engage in battles. They must see each other as enemies.

War invigorates hatred.

War's Goals are Philosophically Unattainable

There are four assumptions in the philosophy of war.

Assumption 1:

Who is a true hero, the one who has perished in war and left behind bereaving loved ones and families or the ones who have survived war? And what is so heroic about dying early or without fulfilling one's potential or leaving behind debt, sorrow, broken hearts and sadness?

Assumption 2:

Isn't calling veterans "heroes" justifying political abuses and extravagance? For one, politicians remain alive while soldiers die. And for another, those who command wars and those who authorize it do not even go to the war zones or war fronts to fight. So, they are afraid to die but they force innocent men and women in uniform to be sacrificial lambs in the name of strategy. In ancient wars, kings led wars, not generals. Kings would justifiably be called heroes because they were not afraid to lay down their lives on behalf of their kingdoms. It is laughable in contemporary times that weak politicians appear to be strong by enacting war legislations and declaring wars while sited in their profligate offices.

War insinuators may be cowards.

Assumption 3:

Death may not be the ultimate punishment or remedy for aggression. To some, death may even be the easy way out, or even a reward for their wrongs. No number of killings in war can lead to unitary depopulation or devastation of one land or group of people; nations are intricately linked.

Assumption 4:

Those who claim to "win" the war, in fact, become more fearful, insecure, unsafe, immobile, and suspicious, than those who "lose" the war. Nations that "win" the war, often, become more bankrupted and may struggle to reconnect or rebuild trust, than the vanquished. The winner is assumed to have spent more on war than the loser.

Often, after the war, the "winner" demands reparations or compensation from the "loser," which is an oxymoron. In the 1930s the Allied Nations demanded war reparations against Germany, but what they had done was to create an Adolf Hitler who superintended over the Second World War. The results were painstakingly catastrophic.

War losses are immeasurable.

Spiritually Senseless

There are four assumptions in the spirituality of war.

Assumption 5:

If those who die in war end up in hell, will they continue to fight or justify war? Assume that you were a general or a soldier in war on earth. You die in war and find yourself in hell. There in hell you find another general or soldier you fought against on earth. What do you do or what was the gain in war? Was war justified or your lives less valued than the war bragging rights?

In war, only evil emerges the winner.

Assumption 6:

If those who die in war end up in heaven, will they hug and embrace those they fought against, or will they love each other? Assume that you are a soldier who died in war while on earth. You come to the gate of heaven and there before you, you see another soldier who perished on the opposite side of the war, probably because of your bullet or sword. What are you going to do? Fight each other again?

Assumption 7:

No-one has ever returned from death, other than Jesus Christ. How do combatants know that by dying in war they know where they will go? Does politics or militarism justify morality? In what spiritual condition do soldiers die?

If, in fact, many soldiers die, they are presented with unholy conditions in camp in which they are exposed to prostitutes, drugs and behaviors that do not glorify God. So, where would they go if heaven is a righteous and holy place? Isn't labeling those who die in war as heroes, in fact, unfair to them in the context of the after-life unknowns?

Assumption 8:

What if the death of a soldier is a direct ticket into hell? Does that mean that the presumption of patriotism is futility?
　　War is patently senseless.

3 | IRRESPONSIBILITY OF WAR

War Avoidance

War must be avoided at all cost, unless not avoiding it is war itself. Indeed, it may be argued that there are times when war is inevitable, and even unavoidable. Take as an example, the killing of innocent Israeli civilians by Hamas in the October 7th, 2023, massacre. In those situations, war may be justified, but only to the extent to which it is proportional. However, as argued, war generates unfettered emotions, and it may become extremely impossible to mete out a just response. So, in all circumstances, war is unjustified, though tolerable.

War must be avoided at all cost.

War Investments

Investment in war is the preparation for war and not for peace. When governments stake hefty budgets in Parliament, they are not preparing for peace, but for war. Only by investing in love, filial, fidelity, and amity will the investment be deemed peace investment. The production of armament and the proliferation of weapons of mass destruction (WMDs) are investments in war, not in peace.

Nations which produce WMDs are advocates for war.

The manufacturing of weapons is advocacy for war, not defense or security. No-one feels secure or safe when a war is declared. Enemies may even be those who are closest to you.

The rise of ISIS, Al-Qaeda and military jihadists in various parts of the world is a challenge. These are non-state actors that use suicide as mechanism for war. These groups, though evil, should not be compared to the declaration of war between or among nation states. It is important that nations unite together and fight mass suicide killers. These groups are the very reason why nations should not declare wars among themselves. It should be the duty of every sovereign state to forge solidarity with other sovereign states and prevent wars or reiterate against non-state aggressors.

It is justified to target jihadists and other violate and violent non-state actors and vanquish them, by any means necessary. Israel, was, thus, justified in targeting Hamas. Civilians, though, must be defended by all parties concerned.

War has never been kind to innocent civilians.

Countries with more advanced weapons eventually experience the worst outcomes of war *per capita* because they necessitate it. Advanced weapons kill fast, quick and precise. In other words, they are efficient and effective. Those who manufacture such weapons necessitate swift killings. However, after wars have been fought, what do those manufactures do or how else would they use excess weaponry for? To be in business, they must continue to produce weapons of war, otherwise, they will be declared bankrupt. So, they must continue to hope that wars continue.

Profit is a rogue motivation for war.

The more brutal you kill others, the worst form of post-traumatic experience you suffer. War is a two-edged sword; no-one engages in war without side effects. When you "win" a war, it means that you kill people. You can't kill people without mental or psychological damage to yourself, no matter who you are. Warring people and nations are mentally unwell.

War may kill the body very fast, but it kills the mind very slowly. And only those who are alive have a mind.

Responsibility for War

Nations and peoples should be responsible for war. There are at least five principal principles against the vagaries of war. These are:

1. Advocacy for amity is a form of altruism.

2. Advanced peaceful coexistence is a universal convention.
3. Atonement for other's aggression is a form of divinity.
4. Arresting and incarceration of warmongers is a universal good and
5. Articulation of peaceful instructions in peaceful times guarantees war avoidance.

Nations and peoples should preach love and not peace, more often than they take a meal. Only love can change warring parties into friends.

When people live together in harmony and solidarity, they are in principle subscribing to a universal convention. They agree not only with words, but with hearts. Such universal agreement can make the world a better place than the discussion or imposition of war.

When a people realize that they have been wronged, it should not be expected that they will let it go. However, it is *divine* to forgive, to let go and to seek other forms of addressing conflicts. This is the meaning of civilization.

All those who insinuate or provoke or begin wars, should be arrested and prosecuted.

It should be a crime against humanity to start wars.

War is against human dignity.

From early, elementary studies, children must be taught to love and not hate, to forgive and not revenge, and to seek peace rather than war. Curricula and instruction guides must provide for amicable resolutions of conflicts. That will lend credibility to the world of tomorrow from the world of today.

Unreasonableness of War

There are at least three principal factors in the unreasonableness of war:

1. Unreasonable in all circumstances
2. Unsustainable in all circumstances
3. Unrealistic in all circumstances

The three principal factors are self-explanatory. It is unreasonable to expect good to come from war. War reasons are unsustainable. People die in war. People have died in war.

There has not been any justification to the reasons why they died. Some, if not most, might have died in vain. War is unrealistic; when people wake up from their anger and grief, they may realize that they did not solve *any* problems with war.

War needs another war to sustain itself.

7 | IRRESPOSABILITY OF WAR

We propose the following nine (9) methods of dealing with war, before it becomes war. When it comes to war, like disease, prevention is better than cure.

Seek to Love, Not Peace

The model that has been adopted so far by the multinational organizations (League of Nations; United Nations, etc.) emphasizes peace and non-violence. This model seeks peace-keeping and peace-making. Peace is good, but love is better.

Peace is Not the Opposite of War

Peace is not the opposite of war, but merely a temporary absence of conflicts. It does not mean that where there is peace there will be no war. War is inevitable in the presence of peace. What holds peace may stumble and break, leading to war. Unless what holds peace is love, war will always be a regular menace among us.

Peace is More Expensive Than War

Peace is more expensive that war, but love is costless. Hence, peace cannot be sustained. Peace is elusive and prone to changing regimes, cultures, emotions, etc. To maintain peace requires enormous amounts of money, effort and investment. There is an economical way – love. When nations love one another, they can fight less and enjoy each other more.

Black Platinum Rule

The Platinum Rule states that, "How you want to be treated is not as important as how the other person wants to be treated." But the Black Platinum Rule states that, "Love seeks for its would-be victim what it seeks for itself if it was a victor." This is not the same as the Golden Rule, thus, "Do unto others what you would like others do unto you." Both the Golden and Platinum rules lack one cardinal ingredient, love. The Black Platinum Rule is a game changer; it is love-centered, and it is sustainable. The Black Platinum Rule can create and preserve lasting peace and it can prevent wars.

Conflict is Necessary to Love

Conflict is necessary to love, but war is unnecessary to peace. This framework is practical. To expect that the desire for peace will produce a world without conflict is a pipedream. Wherever humans are, there are bound to be conflicts. But love is a panacea for a conflicted world. It cures hate and cements grace and amity. Conflicts may be necessary for progress just as it takes friction to ignite a fire. And fire may have both good and bad effects. Conflict is required to produce good effects for the good of humanity.

The End of War is Not the Beginning of Peace

The end of war is not the beginning of peace, but, rather, the ascertainment of enmity. Enemies are former warring parties unless they can love. When peace ends, it can produce a desire for war. Victors may want to fortify their gains by investing further in weapons of war. The vanquished may want to prevent another defeat by pursuing armament and weaponization. It creates a vicious cycle. Only love can end war and prevent further aggression.

And love is free.

Peace is Powerless without Love

Where there is love, there will always be lasting peace, but where there is peace, there is also the possibility of war. Love is necessary for self-control and a dealing in moderation. Peace does not involve the will, but only the process. The very process that may lead to peace, may also be responsible for war. When armistices and ceasefires are not honored and peace treaties are violated, war is inevitable. But love may tramp even on broken promises and violated agreements.

Love never ignores the core of human investigation, which is the good of others.

Love is True Patriotism

Nations go to wars in the name of patriotism. Patriotism is devotion to, and vigorous support for one's country. Patriotism is not blind loyalty. And patriotism can be weaponized against vested interest. One can be very patriotic and still refuse to go to war or take part in war encroachments. Patriots first love others, because it is others who make a country.

Love is the Ultimate Vengeance

If you want to take revenge for yourself or others, love. When you love your enemy, you have truly conquered their hearts. There is no weapon as lethal as love, and no endeavor as sustainable.

Where war fails, love succeeds.

ABOUT THE AUTHOR

Award-Winning, Best-Selling Author, Charles Mwewa (LLB; BA Law; BA Ed; LLM), is a prolific researcher, poet, novelist, lawyer, law professor and Christian apologist and intercessor. Mwewa has written no less than 85 books and counting in every genre and has exhibited his works at prestigious expos like the Ottawa International Book Expo and is the winner of the Coppa Awards for his signature publication, *Zambia: Struggles of My People*.
Mwewa and his family live in the Canadian Capital City of Ottawa.

SELECTED BOOKS BY THIS AUTHOR

1. *ZAMBIA: Struggles of My People (First and Second Editions)*
2. *10 FINANCIAL & WEALTH ATTITUDES TO AVOID*
3. *10 STRATEGIES TO DEFEAT STRESS AND DEPRESSION: Creating an Internal Safeguard against Stress and Depression*
4. *100+ REASONS TO READ BOOKS*
5. *A CASE FOR AFRICA?S LIBERTY: The Synergistic Transformation of Africa and the West into First-World Partnerships*
6. *A PANDEMIC POETRY, COVID-19*
7. *ALLERGIC TO CORRUPTION: The Legacy of President Michael Sata of Zambia*
8. *BOOK ABOUT SOMETHING: On Ultimate Purpose*
9. *CAMPAIGN FOR AFRICA: A Provocative Crusade for the Economic and Humanitarian Decolonization of Africa*
10. *CHAMPIONS: Application of Common Sense and Biblical Motifs to Succeed in Both Worlds*
11. *CORONAVIRUS PRAYERS*
12. *HH IS THE RIGHT MAN FOR ZAMBIA: And Other Acclaimed Articles on Zambia and Africa*
13. *I BOW: 3500 Prayer Lines of Inspiration & Intercession from the Heart: Volume One*
14. *INTERUNIVERSALISM IN A NUTSHELL: For Iranian Refugee Claimants*
15. *LAW & GRACE: An Expository Study in the Rudiments of Sin and Truth*
16. *LAWS OF INFLUENCE: 7even Lessons in Transformational Leadership*
17. *LOVE IDEAS IN COVID PANDEMIC TIMES:*

For Couples & Lovers

18. *P.A.S.S: Version 2: Answer Bank*
19. *P.A.S.S.: Acing the Ontario Paralegal-Licensing Examination, Version 2*
20. *POETRY: The Best of Charles Mwewa*
21. *QUOT-EBOS: Essential. Barbs. Opinions. Sayings*
22. *REASONING WITH GOD IN PRAYER: Poetic Verses for Peace & Unconfronted Controversies*
23. *RESURRECTION: (A Spy in Hell Novel)*
24. *I DREAM OF AFRICA: Poetry of Post-Independence Africa, the Case of Zambia*
25. *SERMONS: Application of Legal Principles and Procedures in the Life and Ministry of Christ*
26. *SONG OF AN ALIEN: Over 130 Poems of Love, Romance, Passion, Politics, and Life in its Complexity*
27. *TEMPORARY RESIDENCE APPLICATION*
28. *THE GRACE DEVOTIONAL: Fifty-two Happy Weeks with God*
29. *THE SYSTEM: How Society Defines & Confines Us: A Worksheet*
30. *FAIRER THAN GRACE: My Deepest for His Highest*
31. *WEALTH THINKING: And the Concept of Capisolism*
32. *PRAYER: All Prayer Makes All Things Possible*
33. *PRAYER: All Prayer Makes All Things Possible, Answers*
34. *PRISONER OF GRACE: An I Saw Jesus at Milton Vision*
35. *PRAYERS OF OUR CHILDREN*
36. *TEN BASIC LESSONS IN PRAYER*
37. *VALLEY OF ROSES: City Called Beautiful*
38. *THE PATCH THEOREM: A Philosophy of Death, Life and Time*
39. *50 RULES OF POLITICS: A Rule Guide on Politics*
40. *ALLERGIC TO CORRUPTION: The Legacy of*

President Michael Sata of Zambia
41. INTRODUCTION TO ZAMBIAN ENVIRONMENTAL LEGISLATIVE SCHEME
42. REFUGEE PROTECTION IN CANADA: *For Iranian Christian Convert Claimants*
43. LAW & POVERTY *(unpublished manuscript)*
44. CHRISTIAN CONTROVERSIES: *Loving Homosexuals*
45. THINKING GOVERNMENT: *Principles & Predilections*
46. WHY MARRIED COUPLES LIE TO EACH OTHER: *A Treatise*
47. LOVE & FRIENDSHIP TIPS FOR GEN Z
48. POVERTY DISCOURSE: *Spiritual Imperative or Social Construct*
49. SEX BEFORE WEDDING: *The Tricky Trilemma*
50. QUOTABLE QUOTES EXCELLENCE, VOL. 1: *Knowledge & Secrets*
51. QUOTABLE QUOTES EXCELLENCE, VOL. 2: *Love & Relationships*
52. QUOTABLE QUOTES EXCELLENCE, VOL. 3: *Hope*
53. QUOTABLE QUOTES EXCELLENCE, VOL. 4: *Justice, Law & Morality*
54. QUOTABLE QUOTES EXCELLENCE, VOL. 5: *Dreams & Vision*
55. QUOTABLE QUOTES EXCELLENCE, VOL. 6: *Character & Perseverance*
56. QUOTABLE QUOTES EXCELLENCE, VOL. 7: *Actions*
57. QUOTABLE QUOTES EXCELLENCE, 1 *of 20*: *Knowledge & Secrets*
58. QUOTABLE QUOTES EXCELLENCE, 2 *of 20*: *Love & Relationships*
59. QUOTABLE QUOTES EXCELLENCE, 3 *of 20*: *Hope*

60. *QUOTABLE QUOTES EXCELLENCE, 4 of 20: Justice, Law & Morality*
61. *QUOTABLE QUOTES EXCELLENCE, 5 of 20: Vision & Dreams*
62. *THE SEVEN LAWS OF LOVE*
63. *THE BURDEN OF ZAMBIA*
64. *BEMBA DYNASTY I (1 of a Trilogy)*
65. *BEMBA DYNASTY II (2 of a Trilogy)*
66. *ETHICAL MENTORSHIP: Missing Link in Transformational Leadership*
67. *AFRICA MUST BE DEVELOPED: Agenda for the 22nd Century Domination*
68. *INNOVATION: The Art of Starting Something New*
69. *TOWARDS TRUE ACHIEVEMENT: The Mundane & the Authentic*
70. *ONE WORLD UNDER PRAYER: For Camerron, Ecuador, and France*
71. *ONE WORLD UNDER PRAYER: For New Zealand, Poland, and Uganda*
72. *ONE WORLD UNDER PRAYER: For Malta, USA, and Zambia*
73. *ONE WORLD UNDER PRAYER: For Germany*
74. *ONE WORLD UNDER PRAYER: For Haiti, Iraq, and Russia*
75. *ONE WORLD UNDER PRAYER: For Chad, UN, and Syria*
76. *ONE WORLD UNDER PRAYER: For Burundi, Canada, and Israel*
77. *ONE WORLD UNDER PRAYER: For China, Egypt, and Venezuela*
78. *ONE WORLD UNDER PRAYER: For Greece, Mali, and Ukraine*
79. *ONE WORLD UNDER PRAYER: For Morocco, North Korea, and the UK*

80. ONE WORLD UNDER PRAYER: *For Belgium, Brazil, and the Burkina Faso*
81. ADIEU PERFECTIONS: *A Satire*
82. OPTIMIZATION: *Turning Low Moments into High Comments*
83. ACING THE IMPOSSIBLE: *Faith in the Other Dimension*
84. END GAME LAW: *Financial Mindset in Quotables*
85. MARRIAGE MAPPING METHODOLOGY: *The Outline of How to Measure the Strength, Love-Condition and Longevity of a Marriage*
86. A CASE AGAINST WAR *The Imperative of Love and Unsustainability of Peace*

INDEX

A

Adolf Hitler. *See* reparations
Africa, 33, 34
aggression, vii, 1, 4, 10, 19, 27
aggressor, 5
aggressors, 17
Allied Nations, 11
Al-Qaeda, 16
altruism, 18
amity, 16, 18, 26
ammunition, vii
ancestors, 3
ancient wars, 6, 10
argument, vii
armament, 16, 27
armistices, 28
assumptions, 9, 12
atonement, 19

B

betrayal, 1
Black Platinum Rule, 25
boomerang, 3
broken hearts, 9
business, 17

C

ceasefires, 28
Christian, 31
circumstances, 20
civilians, 15, 17
civilization, 19
combatants, 8, 13
conflict, vii, 26
country, 29
cowards, 10
credibility, 20
crime, 20
cure, 23

D

damage, 7, 18
dead, 5, 6
death, 3, 10, 13, 14

debt, 9
declarant, 3
declaration of war, 2, 4, 17
declared bankrupt, 18
declaring war, 2
devotion, 29
dignity, 20
disagreement, vii
disease, 23
disputes, 4
divine, 19
drugs, 13

E

earth, 12, 13
Elements of War, 1
embarrassment, 3
emotions, 4, 15, 25
encroachments, 29
enemies, 8
enmity, 27
eternal blessings, 6
evil, 12, 16

F

families, 9

fearful, 11
fidelity, 16
filial, 16
fire, 26
firearms, vii
First World War, 6
flag, 7
free, 27
friends, 19
futility, 14

G

Germany. *See* reparations
God, 13, 34
Golden Rule. *See* Black Platinum Rule
governed. *See* governors
government, 5
governors, 2
guns, vii

H

Hamas, 7
harmony, 19
hate, 1, 4, 8, 20, 26

hatred, 8
heaven, 12, 13
hell, 12, 14
heroes. *See* veterans
hostility, vii
humanity, 20, 26

I

immobile, 11
immoral, 8
incarceration, 19
infrastructure, 7
injustices, 3
innocent, 10, 15, 17
insanity, 6
insecure, 11
insinuators, 10
intrinsic or lasting value, 5
investigation, 28
investments, 16
irrationality of war, 2
ISIS, 16
Israel. *See* Hamas

J

jihadists, 16

justice, 5
justification, 2, 4, 21

K

kingdoms, 10

L

land, 10
law, 31
lawyer, 31
League of Nations, 23
legislations, 10
lose, 11
loser. *See* winner
loss, 7
lost opportunities, 7
love, 29
loyalty, 29

M

militarism, 13
mind, 18
model, 23
moderation, 28
morality, 13
munitions, vii

N

national sentiments, 2

O

opposite of war, 24
outcomes, 7, 17

P

pain, 3
panacea, 3, 26
Parliament, 16
patriotic feelings, 4
patriotism, 14, 29
payback. *See* reprisal
peace, 28
peaceful coexistence, 19
peaceful times, 19
perish, 7
philosophy, 9
Platinum Rule. *See* Black Platinum Rule
politicians, 9
politics, 13
preach love, 19
pressure, 1, 2, 4
professor, 31
profit, 18
proliferation, 16
promises, 28
prostitutes, 13
provocation, 4

R

regress, 7
reparations, 11
reprisal, 5
resolutions, 20
retribution, 6
revenge, 1, 3, 5, 20, 29
Russia, 7

S

sacrificial lambs, 10
sadness, 9
Second World War. *See* First World War
sectarian, 2
seek peace, 20
self-control, 28
senseless, 14
sentimentality of war, 2
sides, 3, 7

soldiers, 9, 13
sorrow, 9
spirituality, 12
Struggles of My People, 31, 33
suicide killers, 17
survivors, 5, 7
suspicious, 11

T

the West, 33
trauma, 7
trust, 11

U

Ukraine. *See* Russia
unavoidable, 15
unholy, 13
unitary depopulation, 10
United Nations. *See* League of Nations
universal convention, 19
unknowns, 13
unpatriotic, 2
unrealistic, 21
unreasonableness, 20
unsafe, 11

V

vengeance, 4, 5, 7
vengeful missions, 6, 7
veterans, 9
vicious cycle, 27
victors, 27
violence, vii, 23
volatile reaction, 5

W

weaponization, 27
weapons, vii, 16, 17, 27
win. *See* lose
winner, 11
WMDs, 16
wrongs, 10

Z

Zambia, 31, 33, 34, 35

www.ingramcontent.com/pod-product-compliance
Lightning Source LLC
Chambersburg PA
CBHW072038060426
42449CB00010BA/2334